# COYOTE WIND

# COYOTE WIND

<>

# Dyana Basist

ELIK PRESS
SALT LAKE CITY

Elik Press Books

© 2018 Dyana Basist

All rights reserved

Cover art by Carolyn Fitz

Special thanks to Jim Jones, as always.

ISBN 9780981856766

765432 First Printing

Elik Press
962 E Lowell Avenue
Salt Lake City, Utah 84102
elikpress.com
ahoffmann@sisna.com

## Contents

<>

coyote versus Coyote   11
Three Haiku   13
The Only Difference   14
Coyote Dreams   16
See How Coyote Shines   18
Praise the Emergency   20
Coyote's Bad Rap   22
Three Haiku   24
I Meet Coyote in the Dollar Store   25
Coyote Under My Skin   26
Carnel Knowledge   30
Turgid Force   32
Habanero Hot   34
Coyote the Great   37
Coyote as Marriage Counselor   39
Three Haiku   41
You and Yours   42
Panicking the Prey   44
Quiet Late   46
Coyote Hunters   48
Coyote on the Mesa   51
Crazy Good   54
Chewing on Grass with Coyote   56
All Day Long   59
Twist: A Haibun   61
The Hunger Moon   63
Medicine Dog   65
Coyote as the Void   66

Acknowledgements

# COYOTE WIND
< >

as if one
lover isn't enough —
coyote wind

coyote vs Coyote

*"Mythology helps you to identify the mysteries of the energies pouring through you. Therein lies your eternity."*
                    Joseph Campbell

My parents moved us to the Tucson desert from Canada the very same year I realized I wasn't a horse. Still, I spent every available moment cantering in the unfamiliar terrain. Hidden springs of water, miles of cottonwood washes. Watched roadrunners spin by, jackrabbits, gila woodpeckers nesting in saguaro. But what grabbed me by my neck's scruff was coyote. In the desert, maybe because the earth's crust was so damn hot, coyote was always loping, her cries as far away, as close as lightning, charged the air, electric.

Not long ago I ended what was ten straight summers in Taos. There was coyote again, always on the move, but trotting. And woven through this whole sacred mess is my life in Santa Cruz with coyote. I have been woken countless times by their squeals and yips, their spring den a hundred yards from my home on Rodeo Gulch, a riparian corridor. When a coyote breaks out into our meadow, rather than loping or trotting, she's sauntering, sleeping in the sun, ears twitching.

In this collection there is a distinction between coyote (the biological animal) and "Coyote the God Dog." I flirt with both. Biological coyotes travel in small packs, mate for life, are good parents, often keeping their young with them up to a year if land allows. A coyote's hearing and smell are so well developed that a sudden noise can change her direction midstep. They are hard runners, twenty five miles an hour, easy, and up to forty. That's damn fast.

Coyote (capital C) the mythic trickster belongs to no one, although all claim him from the Native Peoples to poets, earth lovers and dreamers. We impose our moral values, from our benevolence to our deplorable actions, on this animal like no other. Coyote becomes a Zen master whopping you with a stick. A cheerleader, a perpetrator, a clown bungling with us through our folly. A suspect and a scapegoat. A crucible of searing light juxtaposed to our darkest shadow. Coyote is hostile to fidelity and domesticity. Hit and run. Coyote was there at the beginning, shaping the world, bringing death and fire, and he will be there at the end. A shamanic shapeshifter, he's a total asshole and the ultimate survivor. He's also a she.

So what do coyotes and Coyote have in common? Both are wanderers; they are smart, bold, predatory and elegantly adaptable; running fertile in forty nine states. Hawaii, watch out.

In the middle of the night it's easy to forget who we think we are. Our imagination unfettered, tangled with the splitting howls of the song dogs, we become more like them... free. We've made Coyote the mediator between humans, nature and the divine. Coyote; unpredictable and powerful as flash floods ripping through the desert. The joke's on us.

first spring rain
the young coyote
facing skyward




                                      red tide coyote
                                      coyote looks me up, down
                                      and winks




last to arrive
coyote saunters through
the blossoming gate

## The Only Difference

Two young coyotes circle the meadow
paws crunch on icy grass
their backs frosted winter
muted before the sun.
Bushy tail, black tip dipped in ink.
Some god got even with coyote there.

The male lifts his leg peeing here and here,
stops, while female
sniffs their future:
scent of cat, rat, coon.
Coyote's hungry.

One by one they crawl on thin bellies back
through the blackberry, acacia, willows
disappear into brush.

I want to run out with an offering, maybe
that fat rat that rolled across our roof.
I want to feed coyote
but more, I want to exalt the hole,
entrance to a world, wild with stench
right under my nose in shadows
scraping and snuffling for survival.

I don't want to follow coyote
into the vines, punctured flesh
in a world thick with thorn.

So I just crouch there
squinting into a feral opening
that feeds me
and starves me out.

Trot to the house for a slice of chicken.
The only difference between me and coyote:
the door and the knife.

## Coyote Dreams

No coyote roams on this frozen grass
before the sun comes up.
Coyote's no fool,
nestled up with his sister in winter den.
No one out this early
unless they are hungry or getting paid.
Coyote is neither.

When the sun crests over the willows
coyote smells the temperature change,
smells a cat spraying right at the opening
where he sprayed only last week,
but is too lazy to unfurl, stupid with comfort.

Crack of branch, coyote's eyes snap open, tail flicks
until the combination of silence and a hard-on
drags him back from dreams of catching nine rats,
eating that cat
toying with raven's heart, and flying.
Coyote always wants to fly.

Around noon coyote lazily stretches in the cold sun
shakes off leaves, dirt
and a thousand stolen thoughts.
Trots down to the creek, drinks,
pisses, heads south tracking the rat
easily cornered in dreams.
The cat long gone.

Raven circles above, trailing coyote.
The two tricksters' hearts

linked by love and deceit.
Drops an acorn on coyote's head.

Coyote knows just enough about himself
never to look up.

## See How Coyote Shines

Coyotes are back!
Unable to keep their mouths shut
they howl, shriek, yip, warble
to passing sirens.
The rainy dusk set on fire.

Dogs in the neighborhood go mad
with desire to roam.
People go mad with longing.

Bring in your pets, neighbors.
Stillness hovers in the air like a hawk
but don't be tricked
the full moon is rising.
Pull your blankets tight
keep your windows ajar.
There is no need to wait:
Hormones and howling
will split your skull from dreams,
blasted awake
in the blue mud of dawn.

In the morning
a cat's paw
sticks straight up
in my garden:
back half of a calico
buried among the beets

Coyote jumps straight up
twists in two directions at once

prances, runs in circles
chases its tail
flies up through willow branches after blue jays.
Coyote has wings and bright teeth
wants it all
and in the suburbs
squatting until spring in Rodeo Gulch
the pack will find it.

## Praise the Emergency

Praise the sirens:
fire engines, police, ambulances
that push coyotes to song.
Ears point, necks tilt up
yodel, yip, and whistle
their shrill sutras
punchy prayers
all in answer
to the scream
shocking the urgent air
with its passing emergency.

Sirens as elusive and
fleet of foot to coyotes
as coyotes are to me.

Is it a territorial thing or
are the tricksters
themselves tricked?
Maybe it's just a reason
to blast their harmonies
tangling the quiet.

They taper off. Still one youngster
rattles the neighborhood.
I hear someone clapping.
"Hush," he implores, "be quiet."

I go out to calm things down
with my Tibetan bowl
and soothing murmurs.
Peer into the raveled green.

Coyote ignores me.

I have no idea
what she wants.

## Coyote's Bad Rap

*"Coyotes are tough. They can eat a tin
can and shit out a nail."*
                    Shreve Stockton

Coyote, why is it you have such a bad rap? Your reputation proceeds you. One of lech, trickster, nuisance, all the way down to sinister and evil.

From the Navajo:
   "They say Coyote is funny, some of the people say that. But the old people who told me the stories, they didn't think coyote was funny. Coyote was always causing trouble. He was mean. He caused hardship. He hurt people. He caused people to die. That's the way the stories go, told by my uncles when I was a boy."

Coyote you traverse a well-traveled trail of scorn and fear. From rez to ranch, from rural to urban, you certainly have caused quite a stir. You take what you want, and humans don't like that, right? You like what we like: lambs, calves, pets, birds. You sleep at the edge of dreams in the shadowed bush. And because you are the ultimate omnivore, from scat to cat, you are a shining example of survival of the fittest. You take what's ours, and like all predators at the top of the food chain, we fight back. Humans have proven we will do anything to be top dog, and coyote, you who are just looking for your next meal, have stepped right in it, and out of it and in it, ever since fences and taxes: territory.

Coyote's just hungry. Only humans are rabid with hierarchy and caste. So we dress you up to look like us in cowboy hats and boots, demonize you for strutting your stuff, and try to conquer you. I don't know another animal that has been more anthropomorphized. We can not intern you, or force you into poverty on the reservation. You are stealthy; we cannot control the problem of your wild repertoire. So we exterminate you like the witches. We hang your carcass to rot.

Humans are by nature intolerant and loathe being stolen from, even though we ourselves are masters of the heist. Here's what I think is true. You have outsmarted us, and we hate the competition. We are ravenous for territory, our appetite insatiable. As we pay down our mortgage, tidy our homes, grocery shop, you slide in for the kill and scatter like ghosts to sleep it off in the dirt. Your late-night dirges, your unpredictable behavior, your freedom. You just piss us off. And then piss in our yards.

We will never kill off all of your kind, just like you will never kill off all our sheep. But what we are killing off every time poison is thrown in a den of pups is a part of ourselves. As we divorce the wild, our wild selves disintegrate. The parts of us that squat in the dirt, fingers pushing into the deep mud. Our animal selves. Our howling, keening losses, our twisting with joy successes. Our infrequent repose. All of this adding up to a life, a momentary place on the crusty earth. The earth it would behoove us to share, not just with juncos and chipmunks, but with scruffy coyotes who we will never understand. And give thanks for that.

her toe
glides up his leg
summer dream . . .




blazing heat
he crawls into
the dark ravine




lightning
the loner
coyote

## I Meet Coyote in the Dollar Store

He's wearing black slacks, glossy black shirt, black cowboy hat and sunglasses. Gold cane.

He says, "Ma'am, you have a nice smile," and looks at my ass.

I'm squatting down, searching the rack for reading glasses. "Well, thank you." I flash him my hundred-watt smile and then remember I'm married. It fades to a smirk.

"Darlin', you have a mighty fine day." He turns, tail swishing madly, cane clicks out the door.

## Coyote Under My Skin

    1.
When coyote howls
an eerie wind whips
around my home
grabs the fire pit
hurls it against the adobe
with such force it bends in half.
Lightning glints off his sharp teeth.
He changes the weather
like young men change lovers.

I chant for rain, beg,
lift my shirt to entice the weather gods
but only coyote notices
spins a dust devil
on the mesa's floor
and lobs it at me.

Wind hisses through my heart
and sure, I can run and crank
the windows shut
but wind, like coyote,
will always find a way in.

First monsoon comes down hard
not like war but dance.
Coyote's feet slap the pavement
in a rhythm too fast to make out
in the drum-driven dirge.
Drought ghosts rise like raptors

circle in the white-wine air.
Second rain, coyote drinks before
it hits the ground,
catches hail in his teeth,
would swallow the moon whole
if she only would get close.
Almost did once, when
she rose full like a tostada:

"Moon," he cries, "come closer, so I can
admire you better."
She laughs. "Coyote, you lech, everyone
knows what you did to the sun,
grabbed it from Raven and stuffed it in a box.
Ever since then it's been dark, cold every night."
"Yes, Moon, it's true, but that's why
I can see you better now."
He did have a point.
She came a bit closer.
"Just a little more," crooned coyote, mouth watering.
Precisely then, Raven dives past, bites coyote on the nose.
Moon slips out of coyote's lusty grasp.
Desperate to fly, he tries dancing his way into Raven's heart.
"Loan me your wings, Raven,
and I'll bring you back the moon."
Coyote has learned his best tricks from men.

   2.

Coyote's snout rises above the alfalfa
where he hides, gawks at the prairie dogs
who stand on their hind legs, alert.
He gives up, bored and hungry,

naps, his mouth ajar
two moths fly in
like flute notes sucked back to silence.

His mouth closes and opens again
seven yellow moths flutter out
chase each other
higher and higher until
they become the Pleiades,
a hoof in the night sky.
A lot of work for Coyote to birth stars.
You'd think he'd be able to snag a prairie dog.

   3.

Coyotes gather for a conference.
Tonight they don't howl but chortle, confer,
chatter, confide under piñon and sage,
scatter at dawn...to hunt, to gather.

I lay on my back eating an apple
in the indentation that coyote made in the field.
His fur frames a gravitational pull
around my mammal body.
I wish I were itchy with fleas
thick with indigestion from water
lapped up at the Acequia Madre, mother ditch.

   4.

Coyote winds one black
one white hair
around his tongue
stolen from my pillow.

Dream my yoni is slippery as wet moss.
I go to Ojo Caliente mineral springs
and there's Coyote standing naked
eyeing the girls. I smile, he nods
and like an ember
leaps into me.
I scrub, soak in sulfur water, iron, arsenic
slather three rounds of mud on my body
it dries in the searing sun,
soak as one hundred thousand gallons
of heat steams to the surface.
I scrub and sweat, drink fifty cups of ice water
work hard but to be honest
don't want to get Coyote
out from under my skin.
Why?
Some nights I make love to Coyote when I sleep
and he's the damn sweetest lover I've ever had.

## Carnal Knowledge

Queen Coyote peers through our bedroom windows. A voyeur of sorts, sexologist...curious. She looks for movement but sees none. Her acute ears listen for moans of abandon — silence. A bead of sweat slips down her push-up bra. Coyote, the magician who turns rabbits' feet into jade stalks, is concerned. Women, not all women, but too many have forgotten to have sex, to pleasure themselves, think dirty thoughts that help them sleep in a bed of warm clouds. The Great Forgetting.

Instead they seem to be doing everything else. Women: the gatherers, pick and prune, pickle and put up a thousand dream-jars. But none of them involves smut. And you can't blame the whole shebang on hormones and babies, or no hormones and no babies. It's women of all ages. The millennial to the menopausal, and beyond, not getting any. Coyote wonders why.

They used to sneak vibrators into bed when alone, now snuggle up to cell phones. Check emails instead of their lover's ass. Something better to do than a roll in the hay? She's sure sex is the closest thing to God these animals will ever know. It's the brake pads of life. Get a little feral, invite chaos, pant like a dog. Let it rip.

So Coyote does some thinking and diddling, has seven consecutive orgasms and sleeps for twelve hours straight. Although she may never understand the proclivities of humans, being such a self-actualized slut, she decides to do something about it: sex classes for distracted women.

The Queen of Connection sashays into Good Vibrations in the Mission District of San Fransisco remembering when she used to go there with her girlfriends. Yes, to the back room to try out vibrators together on plush cushioned chairs before the "City" found out and shut it down: unhygienic. True story.

Coyote asks to speak to the manager. Out prances a young green-haired, multi-pierced vixen. Coyote gets her to donate all last year's models of vibrators, butt plugs, dildos, edible lubricant to the cause. She puts up flyers and women come (no pun intended). The class turns out to be a pleasure palace of success. The women reverse The Great Forgetting and start to remember, tell and show others, make love and their multidimensional orgasms set the world smoldering. Robust laughter, slippery yonis, coy deliverances. They feel excellent and beautiful. Sex reminds them to love more. The planet purrs, rolls out lush lullabies. Skin to skin.

So, if you are reading this, Coyote, the Queen of Carnal Amusement, suggests you put this book down and call on your lover or yourself. Push back against the withering machine of separation that tells you you're too busy, too evolved, old, your chest is flat but your stomach isn't. The revolution is under the covers. Get juicy. Get it on.

## Turgid Force

One day First Daughter hears
tap tap tap on her window.
Coyote stands below,
wrapped in a thick Mexican poncho
yellow with black crows.
The dawn glints off his teeth
a pile of pebbles in his palm.
"Come out and play."
"It's too early." First Daughter
slams her window shut.

The next morning and the next
tap tap tap tap tap
dirt gets sprayed on the pane.

On the fourth day
(Coyote knows how to wear a girl down)
he drags her to the
Land of Medicine Buddha.
All the signs point
This Way to Nirvana:
after you boast and grovel
get eaten by the hungry tigress
for a thousand incarnations.
And only until
you lure everyone else
along with you.
Coyote pisses on the Buddha.

They veer off the path
through the steep canyon
the entire redwood forest
hushed with interest.

Coyote points to the trees
hundreds of feet high.
"These are just like
my boner
held rigid by turgid force
columns of liquid.
Yep, that's me."

Coyote has read First Daughter's
weekly horoscope
which says it's an auspicious time
to have an orgy.
"Cosmic clearance" in fact.

She looks up to the engorged trunks
stretching toward sun
to her rapturous hands
at Coyote with his hard-on.

"I'd like to fuck a forest."
Her grin splits the world open.

## Habanero Hot

This is a story that is hard to tell you because it's like admitting you're an alcoholic, would rather drink a shot of tequila than diluted icy with lime juice. But because butterflies only live for six weeks and are floating around my head, and I have fur under my fingernails, I feel compelled to spill it. It's potent because it's about fucking Coyote and that's just plain wrong, isn't it? Sit down, have a shot.

Once upon a time there was a woman. Can you smell her already, Coyote? Your black nose collaring wind, paw poised above the dandelions just beginning to throw their yellow heads above the dirt. Yes, you catch the drift of her and are circling.

This woman was married, had it made, knew it, cherished him and that could be the end of the story. But no, life's too violent and succulent, too despairing and ambivalent for that.

Night after night she wakes to Coyote's thin howls, their barbed sounds spear her heart, but more importantly her vulva, which enlarges like a puffer fish and floats her out to dreams. In these dreams she rides in a scarlet tuk-tuk, careens through motorbikes, towards oncoming traffic, swerves around people, cars. Her driver, his long snout, sharp teeth protrude from his helmet, looks back and winks; feral.

She wakes up in heat, throws off the covers, and sitting at the corner of her bed, the God-Dog taps his alligator cowboy boots on her wooden floor. He reeks; mud and scat, his hands; a rattler poised. She looks at him like he must be kidding. He looks at her like he isn't. Moves in closer, a luxuriant ferocious smile, his breath burns like the desert wind.

Coyote teasing, nips the woman's elbow, the back of her knee, then kisses her directly on the mouth, hard. Bleeding lower lip, faint growl. Her hands on his flanks, his nose sniffing, always wary, ready. Licking her breasts, belly, twirling. She sucks and bites him, stunned snarling. Sweat trickles down her neck. Parting pubic hair, shudders, coyote gently places his nose on her vaginal petals and lifts her. She opens, her cunt a hot spring, sulphur slippery. In and out and then flips her, engorged, and swallows her whole and she him. So slow, so fast, so soft and now increasing, they fuck each other to the moon. Because isn't that where these kind of love stories live anyway? Free from gravity's pull.

And just like that this story is told, fleshed out, exhausted. The woman imagines Coyote sprawled in a warm thicket, sleeping off his late night, bad-ass take down. In the deepest dark, strains to hear his distant whistles, or maybe a rubbing of trees, she can't be sure. Flea bites circle her ankles like bracelets. She stalks him with words. Scatological.

As for Coyote, he's long gone. Never one for fame or fortune, he's much more akin to Don Julio straight up. Still, he remembers her tangled hair pitched back in pleasure. How she smells like hummingbirds thick with nectar. Sometimes when marking his territory he passes her window, furtive in the dark. Stops to chortle, howl himself into her salty sinew. Heartbreaking gypsy songs of old.

Survival songs. Creation songs. He gives her this; she who dreams him hard.

## Coyote the Great

A female Coyote, the magical priestess of all things naughty, saunters by a statue of Sita Devi, the Queen of Chastity, and laughs. Coyote's a slut, takes no cash, does the whole thing on trade. Loves to swagger her stuff, flaunt it. Sex addiction — such a human concept. Why wouldn't you want to fuck yourself stupid? Carnal knowledge, animal like.

Coyote stands at the corner of Broadway and Eighth, any city or town. Your town, your city. Kelly-green short shorts, blue thigh boots, lace bodice. Hair, lots of it, tawny soft like corn tassels to her waist. Sea-shell earrings lit by the moon. Blood red lips and polished teeth. Coyote's horny, a real bitch. In heat.

This mistress of the night, she will howl you a hard-on and take you, cuddle you, or nail you to her fleshy walls. She will lick you until you cry or slap you silly. She will blow you or watch you blow. Steal your heart, your wallet, with aromatic incantations.

But there's one thing she will never do and that's be there when you wake up from your spent stupor. The queen of wily wandering, where is she going? Is that her running dogs into the ground, wailing rapturous at dawn?

The ultimate multi-tasker, Coyote's long gone to her clan. Her pups, getting too big to keep in the den. Fierce for their survival, next week she'll start teaching them to stroll, hunt. In your neighborhood.

*

So, does it work for you, dear reader, coyote being a sexy she dog? If Coyote is the God-Dog and God is a woman, doesn't it follow that she is the Goddess? She snorts at this thought. All these omniscient human notions, damn tiring. Still, why do males have all the air time, even in the mythic? Imagine being a little bit badder? No matter your age, strut with her, break some rules. Don't you just want to drive your convertible off a cliff with her thumb in your ass? What a seraphic siren, it's all in that sidelong smile.

## Coyote as Marriage Counselor

Coyote does not suffer fools. And fools these humans tend to be. She will never understand why after a short period of fabulous fornication, they create lavish weddings that hinge on just seven words. The first vow, "I do," snares these fickle fleshy couples. I do? You do and then you don't.... What could be more obvious? Then there's how she makes her living: "Till death do us part."

Coyote loves her job, makes a killing as these innocents often turn rivals, stoop to every nasty and underhanded trick. They cheat, lie, withhold and hold out in an attempt to assert their independence, and then try to save that same sacrosanct union.

A sheen of anticipatory sweat breaks across Coyote's forehead as she smells her clients enter the building. She meticulously cleans and shines her long nails, then pulls back her curly mane. Squeezes into a conservative, tight pencil skirt, the fitted jacket showing her ample cleavage. Jimmy Choo pink pumps. Crosses her legs and waits.

The couple marches into Coyote's darkened office, the acrid odor of anger trailing after them. Humans, so delicate and dense, paying her obscene sums of cash to get last week's drama spun into this week's insights. She sighs at their endless escapades. Advice adverse, they never get it. And never will. She watches the woman extract a stick of gum, exuding disdain.

Looking intensely interested, Coyote snickers to herself, reweaving the spider's web. Compassionate, like peering through brush at a rabbit trembling in the grass. The man notices a dribble of saliva oozing from Coyote's pink lips. Watching the woman's fine calves, the man's biceps, Coyote's eyes glaze over as she thinks back to the rabbit, paralyzed, before the pounce. The counselor shakes herself back to the matter at hand.

Coyote waits for one of them to speak. A tactic that always shifts the power balance in her favor. She can wait all day. Coyote is very patient.

watching coyote
the windowpane chills
my nose



autumn tryst
white waves pulling me
closer



the last guest leaves —
coming out to frolic
coyote moon

## You and Yours

All week smell of cat urine
sprayed at my front door
and yesterday bobcat
saunters across the yard
looks back once
conveying "strong, well-fed, easy."
I am delighted to be tagged.

Today coyote hops up from rest
tilts pointed ears forward and waits
front paw poised delicate.
Feels the gopher under nose.
Frozen for twenty minutes
leans forward, chin to grass
then sniffs the air,
shrugs shoulders, circles for
another nap in the shade.

Coyote and I sleep together.
Me in bed, he in the meadow below.

I've been so tired lately and blame it on
his kind.
They explode into the night: chortle, yap, howl
partying with the pack, like teenagers
who think no one can hear them,
or better yet, could care less.

But last night it didn't sound like a party.
Rather a furred keening burst the silver shadow
as I woke stunned, hunting meaning.

This lineage of longing and belonging
that we animals marry into;
not quite warm enough
then sweaty too hot.

So it's you: coyote and bobcat
and even the garden spider I've claimed
careful not to disturb, though I'm shocked
every time she stuns, winds prey
and sucks her meals flat.
I put my money on you and yours
the stalk and stench,
although as I watch the world unravel
I know all bets are off.

## Panicking the Prey

Coyote, no sirens tonight,
so why out of absolute quiet
does the pack explode
like banshees?

So close, I vault up
snap lights off
slip out, squat on my deck
want to decipher
your barbaric a cappella
building to a bold crescendo.

Startling silence.

It's called "panicking the prey"
when hunting, in pursuit
the pack goes crazy;
barks, whines, howls from all sides.
A disorientation of searing song.

Rabbit brought down, the dirge cuts off like death.

Then rustling:
I squint to see you
and you and you
sliding like scruffy moons
through the brush.

Far to the east
another pack;
their thin violinic replies
mapping each other's warm flanks

I want to lie down
in the shadow meadow
and am afraid.

## Quiet Late

Stars flicker through slatted fog,
takes forever to fall asleep. Still,
coyote, I'm glad to be shocked
from night's blind arms
to hear teens in the park
across the corridor baiting you,
howling drunk.

You and the pack start up, bellow and shriek.
Rip a hole down the seam of that party,
shut those big boys down.

Very late

I jolt to wake, screams
of a forgotten dog, its life
ends in your strong jowls.

The edge of night, I suck
in the good air
the violence and certainty of
the pack being fed.

Quiet late

Scan the frontier
we steal from the wild.
Intersection between
my human neighbors
and the feral ones.
I don't blame you, coyote.

I take heart in your hunger
your exhaustive demonstrations.

The boys go home and
remember to bring in their dogs.
I spill to sleep, lucid with longing.

## Coyote Hunters

They call them "yotes"
in hunting and survival magazines,
distancing the rifle from the prey.
Hunters chide and taunt each other
for wearing full sniper "camo" or not:
"My grandfather dusted 'em in nothing more
than jeans and a t-shirt."

Another gentleman suggests,
"You take coyote liver, spleens, lungs,
pour blood over it and
freeze it in a five gallon bucket.
Smack it upside down
and out slides
a 'yote-popsicle'
watch to see them come in
for a whiff." Bang!

Run coyote,
you, our fastest carnivore,
run and hide
like women, blacks,
like gays, Indians.
Stay low.
The hunters, they string up
carcasses on their garages
like scalps.

Stinking satisfied they
knock down a cold one
knock up their women.

But when they sleep stupid
we will saunter stealthily
into their dreams,
won't we coyote?

We will make them eat
their spent metal slugs
until their intestines twist
like ocotillo in drought.

And then we'll go dancing
you and me, coyote, because
we remember the old trails
that arc like veins
in the bush,
the barking songs
that keep the litter strong.

We will paint the town red.

frost on scat —
where are we going
this time, coyote?




weather maker —
slips while conjuring
the city graupel




coyote
let's forget about death
river of stars

Coyote on the Mesa

1.

Coyote stops by Orlando's for fish tacos
smothered with green chili,
tired of crickets and crows,
all this skulking around.

Reads the Taos News blotter
while sucking on bitter juniper berries:
a caller reports two people hitting
each other with corn cobs;
a resident reports a trespasser mowing their lawn;
intoxicated man reported attacking
a woman with a tube of lipstick
after she was caught feeding his dog.
Possible wolf sighting.
Ten cows on the road.
Two aggressive bulls,
white horse on the run.
Coyote gets a headache,
trots outside, stands at the corner
directing cars into each other
crash crash, plucky and modern
more fun than scattering rabbits.

2.

Coyote is building a new house directly behind me
screwing with my sunset view.
I climb over three barbed wire fences
to talk to the builder.
"I live there." Pointing east to the adobe

with the portal and hammock.
His worker, the shaved one covered with tattoos,
glares at me. "How long you lived here?"
" Seven years," I pipe up proudly.
"Moises Martinez and his family...seven hundred."

3.

One morning Coyote scuttles on my dirt road past Chato
who is chained in the heat. No exercise,
little water, depressed. Never friends, Coyote used
to be wary when the dog was free to wander
but now it's vile to watch.
Coyote sees the little girl jump
on her trampoline, back flips, front flips.
he swaggers out of hiding
in red cowboy boots and a low brim hat,
tries to lure her into the bush; she's tender, tasty.
She doesn't notice Coyote's lewd gyrations.
Later Coyote sees the boy running in the field while
Chato goes crazy, throat pulled taut by chain.
The boy never bends to pet him.


Of course Coyote knows the problem is the father
and the father's father
whose heart got lodged in his trachea.
The Spaniards still stink like
conquistadors. Now they conquer the wood pile
splitting head after heathen head.
Coyote slips under the fences down to the Morada
spies on the Penitentes who whip themselves
among backyard fences,
still yes to this day.
Some humans believe only they have souls

but Coyote knows this to be dangerous.
Once saw a horse lie down in grief when its partner died
heard a tree cry when it was cut
hears mountain ache with his ear to the scree.
Coyote leaves a dead rat for the dog, who
ignores the gift, waits patiently for his kibble.
Coyote pisses on the double-wide's porch. Again.

## Crazy Good

Coyote, my collaborator
my panic and prey
you're the berry vines that
rip my ankles and won't heal
as I track your hasty retreat.

Coyote, furred daemon,
you're the furrow where I plant seeds
that grow to fifty pound pumpkins
in the thin dirt
the hem of my skirt that keeps
unraveling.

Oh, great smuggler
your lawless song floats
like willow seeds
swirling.

Coyote, I'm burning up
why did you tell me
that chili pepper was mild?

I wait for you in the dark
you slip through
my
fingers
like
kelp.
We can live forever, come on
give me asylum in your den.

Tell me, am I just another piece of ass
well, am I?

I'm waiting.

## Chewing on Grass with Coyote

**1.**
Dusk in the meadow;
clean sweep of green.
Young coyote stands
in the back corner
umber in the darker shadows.
She looks stunned to have stumbled
out of the bush
into all this open.

Sniffs, chews the long grass
and I remember also eating grass
by the railroad tracks in Peru in 1980.
Lugging around the New Age bible:
*Survival into the 21st Century*
which said starving
was necessary for awakening.
A fast of grass and watermelon
at the Urubamba River,
the ankle of Machu Picchu.

Instead of enlightenment
we got ripped off.
Asleep outside the mud hut,
ours for a dollar a night.
Must have sent a child
through the tiny window,
our lock still on the door.

The next morning,
no hiking boots, no Swiss army knife

or clothes, gone. They left the book
and a valley of grass . . .

Coyote continues to munch,
trots on the arc path
probably made by her kind.
Invisible till now, but every day and night
they go wild with the sirens
ten of them, maybe more
A sing-song of grief
and cheer that I inhale
like a mantra
to right my world
tip the balance
to get me closer to God.

     2.

I'm coming to terms that
people come and go.
My lover who followed me to Peru
left me to walk into the Andes
in search of Vilcabamba,
the mythic paradise of the Inca.
Ended up with dysentery instead.

Coyote, my lover.
God-dog squints
into the sun and winks
then swallows the moon.

Someone told me I had written
enough coyote poems,
followed too much scat.

I say, fuck you.
As long as coyote comes
I will snatch her stench
and streak it across the page
like shooting stars.

That's what poets do:
we listen, we watch hard
and scrape harder
to get to the underbelly.

Coyote's sleek fur: chestnut, rust, silver,
vanishes into the dark
and I wonder how just one sighting
of one golden trick dog
can be enough to renew my faith
in the good?

## All Day Long

All day coyote sleeps in the meadow.
I usually see him for a few moments
prancing, nosing around
but today, different.
My partner says coyote is sick
but I say he's tired.
Tired because my mother is here
and she can't get off the couch.

All day long coyote and my mother sleep.
She dreams of dancing
partner fleet of foot and handsome.
Coyote dreams of hot sun,
killing cats.

The world is so busy
that coyote needs to sleep us off
just to breathe radiance back into fur.
My mother sleeps to shake off too many deaths
gathered around her feet like autumn leaves.

They dream and my partner sweeps.
Bamboo leaves slip around the broom
he doesn't give up.
He likes the piles and how it all ends
with nothing.
Coyote likes nothing and how it all ends
with piles.
My mother likes neither.
At the same instant coyote and my mother
wake up, groaning .

Coyote stretches long, slides in to the bush.
My mother hauls her torpid body up the stairs
one insulting step at a time.

Leaning on broom, wind gusts,
my partner starts crying the tears
of ten thousand jobs well done,
in a world
that could care less.
Ten thousand piles
completed
and completely forgotten.

## Twist: A Haibun

Coyote sightings always come with a twist.
The last one involves two ticks.
We stroll the fields at dusk
spring flowers pink and yellow
and there's a coyote
legs dip like ladles in waist high grasses,
trots leisurely, poker-faced,
looks back once, gone.

"Do you always see coyotes?" my friend asks.

"Yeah, saw one earlier today.
Watched three crows in the willows
badgering a hawk
while coyote drowses in the sun
opens one eye,
tilts snout up to the row
unmoved."

My friend calls me later.
"Found two ticks.
You better check."

I strip
in front of my husband
he checks my neck
my silver hair
like a river of clouds
lifts my breasts
tiny pinch of nipples

index finger traces my spine
squats to circle my ankles.

He checks and checks
and then we forget about checking
while coyote, eyes shining
hears our muffled clamor
looks back once, gone.

                fat coyote
                legs up and laughing
                Indian summer

## The Hunger Moon

Coyote, my tether to trust
hot line to hope
my pipe dreamer, jaunty jack-ass
my ace in the hole,
tough guy, homeboy,
no green card or papers.

Is that you skulking
in the bruised dawn
yapping outside my
bedroom window?

You've outlived months of
the driving rains, floods,
now beyond all reason
circle your ancestral
den of decades.

I've missed you;
how the dark moon
waits for her sun.

Won't you stay
oh wandering minstrel?
Keep me up at night
sing your bawdy tales
howl me to health.

Take me coyote
the way stone is caressed

and cracked by the
same waters.

Helplessly wet, I'm yours.

## Medicine Dog

*"We are animals. When we pretend to be something better, we become something worse."*
David Gessner

I run outside when the daytime sirens become coyotes' howls. After the torrential rains swept away their twenty-year den, the pack is back. Farther north, but still in the riparian corridor which borders my home: Rodeo Gulch. And what a rodeo it is.

I want to howl; pull their song in like medicine to strengthen my thinning bones, calm my rebellious thyroid. God, I have missed them. When they abruptly end, I stand barefoot in the grass. My world slightly less wobbly and hopeless.

I breathe in coyote, I breathe out fear. I breathe in coyote, I breathe out grief. And when I breathe in again, I start shaking like a dog. A moan escapes, a whimper, a growl. I'm on all fours under the willow trees. Push fingers into the dampness. Feeling under this thin crust of soil to the mycorrhizal filaments as this nutrient web criss-crosses through the earth. I can hear whispers curl into me.

A dragonfly wings by. The taste of honeysuckle wafts through the air. I roll and transform into a beast, one I know well, and don't know at all. The Other. Lips quiver, teeth exposed, head cocked. I can feel coyote river into my bones. My skeleton, a tuning fork, reverberates though the dry corridor brush.

## Coyote as the Void

She slips out of her dungarees and pressed white blouse. Folds them carefully, pulling off her wedding ring, then her watch that has stopped telling time long ago. Holds the back of her earrings while disengaging the silver posts. Cowboy hat with the silver conch, tipped off her head. Last, unlaces the boots, her toes wriggling free. Lays everything gently on the red rock knowing she will never put them on again.

It is a star-filled night in the desert. So different from the city where she lives. But tonight, no sirens, no disagreements, no, not out here. Just the wind twisting her sliver hair in coils. Faint rustlings. Between this life and the next there is work to be done and god knows she is diligent, dogged even.

She hears a coyote howl, the sign she has been waiting for. The hairs on her arms electric, she shivers in anticipation of what lies ahead. Another howl closer, then another. The coyote's howls coming one after another like contractions when she gave birth to her son so long ago. She looks up to the crescent moon, this glorious life. And now she looks down to see the coyote staring straight at her. Unafraid, neither predator nor prey — equals. His yellow eyes to her brown. The circle has been cast long ago.

The coyote turns, trots into the crackling cool night and she follows. They weave their way off the desert floor effortlessly. Up the red rock mountain where stones murmur in celebration of their passing. She can hear the water now pulling them forward. Follows the stream gathering force, driven river-snake. As she crests the top, the roar of the waterfall at her feet blasts through her skull severing all debris, memory and finally all desire.

The woman is innocent, lovely. Coyote waits. Neither this nor that. No right or wrong. A great happiness pulses through the woman's body as she walks up to the coyote. Runs her fingers like an incantation through the scruff of his neck. The coyote smiles, gets up and starts loping, paws splayed like wings, right over the cliff's edge, into the void. There is only one thing to do. She has been waiting her whole life for this. She runs and dives. Her body straight as a silver- starred arrow, following the howling throat all the way down.

disappearing
into the long night
shadows

# Acknowledgements
—

I want to thank my sisters in our long-lived Seven Stars writing group. You have heard every one of these poems, cheered me on, cried with me and for me. To Marilyn Duhamel, may the fox keep coming to your window, nose to nose. I could not have done this without you.

A few years ago I stumbled into haiku. Because of the Yuki Teikei Haiku Society of California, I have learned and flourished. Bows to our Dojin, Patricia J. Machmiller, whose generosity continues to astonish. She looked at every haiku in this book.

Thank you to the talented Carolyn Fitz, haiku poet, calligrapher and ink artist, who designed the cover, even when I told her it would bring her neither fortune nor fame. inkstonefitz@comcast.net

Deep gratitude for my long road friend, editor, publisher, and stunning writer Andy Hoffmann of Elik Press. Hands in the dirt, eyes to the horizon.

Bows to my small, potent circle of friends, for the truth and deep affection. To my sis, Stacey, this long life . . . . To my son Aza, for holding my hand, jumping off that high rock into the Rogue River. We made it.

To my partner and greatest fan, Leaf Leathers, who decades ago agreed that we were solid enough for me to have a long-term affair with coyote. He has taught me how to love. Coyote digs that.

I was always a bit superstitious that when I finished a book on coyote, the dog would disappear, medicine with her. But early this winter morning I went out to snag a last fig and there was a big pile of scat on the path. Had to step over it. How do I know it was coyote's? It was filled with my figs.

To coyote, you have stretched me. Riotous may you roam.

< >

To contact Dyana Basist about coyote, haiku, or other lyric poetry:
openmesa@sbcglobal.net

Elik: one who has eyes